What I wanted to do

      was take everything I knew

      music, theatre, poetry, and dance

and I went out

      and found everything I could find

      that would make a noise!

      And now

      I'm Marco UnderSong

All true poetry is an invocation to the goddess

GEKKER PUBLISHING

Copyright © 2024 by Marco UnderSong

Published 2024 by Gekker Publishing

http://gekkerpublishing.com

Seattle, WA 98118

First Edition

Printed in the United States

Cover design © 2024 by Gekker Publishing, photo of Marco UnderSong

Post-cover headshot by Jimo Perini, photo of Marco UnderSong, Leland Hotel, San Francisco (circa 1977)

Next image: Marco UnderSong, "Dancing in America"

All photography from the UnderSong Archive

ISBN-13: 979-8-9918840-1-3

THE BOOK OF UNDERSONGS

By Marco UnderSong

Contents

RAINBOWS

Your rainbows

will be blotted out

by the wrath of the coming darkness

Pitiful creatures   left to rot

in the loam

of your own illusions

We do not stand at the threshold

of a new dawn

of a new beginning

We have walked

hand in hand

thru the doors of a twilight

Angels walk with us

The way is long

and the wind is cold

THE ISLE OF YOUTH

We

who have loved and lost

and wept in Sorrow's soft silence

as waves of pain

crested and broke

on the shores

of the Isle of Youth

have touched truth

Celestial and solitary

we move motionless

in the Rounds of Time

Encased in crystal carbon

All fallen angels

cast from heaven

to bestow

An end to beginning

Number the days

we die

Dry poisoned berries

Evil flowers

plucked from

the Vines of Violence

LULLABY

In confusion

the song remains true

And magic is the lullaby

of contentment

in rhythmic motion

To pass through time

is our honor

So let us wrap ourselves

in eiderdown

And make love on

green and blue

NEW ORLEANS

In this land of paved grey

      where no eye views the Milky Way

I lay my body down to rest

Shot to hell to kiss the Sun

      I'm leaving from this frozen land

      I've come to New Orleans

      I've come to New Orleans

The unseen is all around

    especially in this place

Nemesis comes to exact her due

    a perfect place in space

I've come to New Orleans

    to lay my weary body down

OBSERVATION ON A GIRL

The sickle of time

Shall cut a large swath

Through shared moments

There are Kings

and pawns

Always!

And the hum drum numbness

of our day to day toil

But of love?

How can we know?

Those born high

And those of lowly birth

Are the same in this

We,

The Envy of Angels

Are Birds of Passage

THE SONG

The Snakes hissed into the Dragon's ear

    "We know your hurt

        that's why we're here

Please share with us

your loss and pain

        and we'll give back to the Bard to

sing"

    So the Snakes were sent

Along their way   (Into the

Milky Way)

To carry "the Song"

Into another day

But the Dragon roared

And cursed the gods

Who would leave him alone

As Love's Earthly guard

NOVEMBER MANIFESTO

I shall not seek

reelection nor resurrection

I yield to all!

And in my stillness

I sit enthroned above and outside

all law

SEATTLE COFFEE

A gaggle of office girls

And the din

of noisy traffic

The post-lunch laughter

of work

On a Tuesday afternoon

I'm not a morning person

And the one single thing

That separates me from

The Great Mass of

humanity

is my nocturnality

I love the night

And my life begins

after dark

ONCE UPON A TIME

The Day

    will surely come

The Night

    will always end

And down

    the halls

        of laughter

            Memories begin

Goodbye

      to all my lovers

Goodbye

      to all my friends

Goodbye

      to all my sorrows

           until we meet again

Hello morning sunshine!

Hello blue sky!

      (There was you and I

           Once upon a time)

ONLY A GHOST

Oh

    Woe to us

        Now that

The States

    are gone

Only a ghost to hold the night at bay

    The mad dog's throat

    was slashed

by the states

Every virtue is in ruin

Every farm deserted

Every fruit

Every flower

All the birds

A confederacy

of iron and will

Forged with hope

Cruelly smothered

by sheer numbers

and new ideas

SCOTLAND

I run

    through the hills

And pick flowers

    in that land of stillness

Oh White Rose...

    I will stop

        and smell

            the flowers

REALM OF EPOCHS

Far to the North

Beyond the sea

Lies a land of the dead

A land of solid water

Where shades commence

The Lady of Ice

carries the seed

of the Sun and her

Mother Earth and in

cold stillness

moves

In this Realm of Epochs

Consciousness is the recollection

of the Knowledge of our

ancestors

We are in a Holy place

pause and be humble

Our father is angry

and our mother is tired

Oh sisters and brothers

    let them rest

Behold them asleep in one another's arms

As lovers in youth

    The eldest of passing winter

rejoices in their

    eternal relationship...

WALES

In the beleaguered

Hills of Wales

We bore

And we buried

The seeds of discontent

We locked away

The Fading Day

In stone cold grey slate

And carved our names

Over

Caernarvon

Roman Boulevards

Neolithic Causeways

And

The promise of Salvation

Turned us South

To the smokey December

Coalfields

of countless invasions

Light a candle

And say a prayer

For those

        buried alive

By earth or by sky

Oh bitter black bruise

      The true Daemon Flowers

Lie sleeping

      In ten thousand holes

Upon the grey green arms of Wales

BE ON TIME

The constellations

       dip and bow

and parade across

      the great night

Breathe deeply and sigh

      Look back

        towards

the setting Sun

And think of me

Bless my soul's Journey

Because of you

I don't go alone!

We will meet again

On the head of a pin

My lover

My friend

Be

On

Time

THE BOW

Dressed and painted in ragtime

The rabble theater

Takes a bow

The stilted applause

drifts down

red burnished balconies

And blesses those below

BRANDED

Two lovers

are

Tranquility and Solitude

And Melancholy

soothes my longings

In this blue black December

where pressed flowers

in occult books remember

Sex sears

like a slave brand

And bonds in a fiery chalice

of Ecstasy and Enchantment

UNIMPRESSED

(RETREATING THROUGH THE SNOW)

There comes a time

when you're not impressed

Is that death?

No! It's just the loss of passion

But it is death on a certain plane

barbed-wire

Retreating through the snow

The freezing fall behind

The horror of madness

(for it comes for each of us)

The sadness

is overwhelming

And we age perceptively

We are retreating through the snow

The freezing fall behind

The dull repetition of

engaging voices

My loves mingle

on my periphery

And I am freezing...

LOVE STREET

I need to go back

    To Love Street

Just one more time

    And remember

        holding your hand

On a warm San Francisco night

I need to walk

The cold grey streets

        of Olde London Towne

Along the muddy river

        they call Thames

I need a train somewhere

        I've never been

I want to fall in love again   Please

OBLIVION

The touch of wind

    And

    The taste of rain

Are in your laughter

        and your clothes

        and I could see

            Her majesty

In the newly fallen snow

    But in between

The Murder of Eden

And the Death of an Angel

There lies

A faltering new beginning

Hands

and lips

And souls depart

On their own Ragged Journey

Toward feebleness and oblivion

PRIMROSE HILL

December's children

Now be still

A flower wilts

On Primrose Hill

And like a bird

In a golden cage

She fills

Her days

With little things

Like sorrow

POPPIES

She is standing

in the morning rain

Is she coming round again?

from a million miles away

I thought

I heard her call my name...

Poppies grow

on concrete hills

The streets are full

of strung-out girls

Move along

He'll be back round

Wrap yourself

in eiderdown

Raw sienna

and other shades of brown

she'll be back round

Paint your nails

in tarmac black

She knows the signs

of the zodiac

She can tell you

who you are!

By the stars

and

tarot cards

GHOST TRAIN

There's a ghost train

    that arrives here at midnight

With the same passenger

    every time

She arrives at the station

        drawn by six white horses

And the hounds of hell

    are at her side

And the sky

    cracks open

        here at midnight

When she lets her long hair

        come tumbling down

There's a ghost train

    that arrives here at midnight

And the lion

    and the lamb

Shall both

    lie down

THE PAST

The past dances

      in a dream

As all the ballet sleeps

      nothing to hold

      nothing to keep

Like a shipwreck

      on a concrete beach

Oh heaven

is just a chance

that we take

I'll hold your hand

if you stay awake

Oh my baby blue

this world is killing you

Fire is Fire

no matter!

Whether it consumes

the witch or the martyr

Flout yourself

Disown yourself

Scream!

Flutter into the flame

and burn your

wings...

ONE TRUE LOVE

I remember

    that tender age

Our

    adorable time

        My Angel of Heaven

    from

    Seven to Eleven

Like a thorn on a rose

Like a long time ago...

They say

you just get

one true love

I hope that's not true

Because if you just get

One true love

My one true love

was you...

EPONA

We ran

    like

        ponies

Through

    the

        woods

And

through

the fields...

And you tied your hair

in a ponytail

above

the Golden Gate Bridge

MADISON

One winter

    when we were young

On Christmas eve

    we made love

The ice in the trees

    shines in the Sun

    like diamonds

I went for a walk

    this Christmas day

And thought of friends and family

    and faces that were changing

        far away

Friends and lovers

    where have you gone?

Is the world so large

    we can't go on?

        I've looked for all of you

            (and every clue)

One last look around this town

on Christmas day!

CHINESE SQUARE

Far away

On the shores

of silence

A weeping Lady

Mourns the passing

of day

Silver cloud

Sewn on my coat tail

Love and laugh

And dream

In a Chinese square

Bloody crime!

Tainted tomorrows

    Bury my heart

    In a Chinese square

Men-at-arms

    Tidings of sorrow

Bury my heart

    In a Chinese square

—May 1990

PLATES

ZOO MUSIC GIRL   (Minneapolis cemetery)

Photo by Michael Boer, ZOO MUSIC GIRL (University of Washington)

Band poster, THE UNDERSONGS (The Haight, San Francisco)

THE UNDERSONGS *(Mabuhay Gardens, San Francisco)*

Photo by Jimo Perini, THE UNDERSONGS   (San Francisco)

Marco UnderSong, Christoph Gladis, Kevin Lavely, & Luke Feldman

THE FLOWERS OF EVIL   (on the road)

Marco UnderSong performing with BLACK ATMOSPHERE

(Seattle)

*Marco UnderSong, model Rachel Kaltenbach *Joyous Gard**

*Marco UnderSong *Dancing in America**

*Marco UnderSong, model Rachel Kaltenbach *Joyous Gard**

TUESDAY

Traffic's a gas

On the open road

December Sun

On smokey white

A whistle sounds

And go to work

Only reminded

Of my regrets

Metal wind

    In the golden light

Cross the Thames   Cross the

Mississippi

To London town   To old St. Paul

    Chords that shock

    The coming wave

        Someone reminds me

          It's Tuesday

Streets that reach

    To open sky

      Golden fields

        Of wheat and corn

Dreams that seek

Another way

Someone reminds me

It's Tuesday...

ROUND & ROUND

Do you think

      it's alright

If we met

      one more time

     so I could

        look into

          your eyes

And say "I'm sorry"

You know it would be OK (at the end of the day)

Nothing would change

You were the best I ever had

Round and round

it goes

Where it stops

No one knows

But there is always

One last time

Do you remember then?

Yes I do remember when

I never felt stronger in my life

I never felt

        more alive

ENGLISH ROSE

It used to be

when I was young

I held an English Rose

But my heart

was broken

so many years ago

Now all the party girls

with their sunshine eyes

blink away the tears

It's raining...

FOR ALLISON

Such a waste

    of time

To blame our troubles

    on love

Endless glasses of wine

Two lovers played with the night

Torn paper hearts

Pressed between the pages

of all the could have beens

Anne is sleeping

once again

Now it's over

the hills

And through

the woods

She's climbing

the mountain sides

(She sighs)

Anne is sleeping

once again

And there's a full moon

over Virginia

HOUNDS

Of all the friends

I've ever known

You stand alone

We were hounds

that ran through

the lilies

of the valley

And I've often wondered

If you ever took a lover

That was half

What I was...

DEATH'S TOUCH

It is a fearful thing

    to love

        what death can touch

At the ivory arches

    of the palace

We tied her to the throne

Oh herald!

The Queen is coming

In silver

blue

and gold

It is a fearful thing

to love

what death can touch

THE BAND

Pause with me a moment

I have a story to tell thee

    I bide here not for long

    So please hear me

Oh once

    I was Golden

See my tatters now

    Down the columns of Ages

I have come

We shall walk

    through fields and meadows

And make love

    by the sea

And cry

    in grief and sorrow

at the loss

    of what could have been

Oh once

    I was Golden

See my tatters now

    Down columns of Ages

I come to tell you now!

Though the sky turn black

And the stars fall down

    Though we breathe

    a poison breeze

They will sing of us

    in times to come

        This I know will be

THE SEVENTH DAY

On the seventh day

The three

of them

The woman and two men

Wandered through the ruins

And ate a dog

GALSWINTHA

Galswintha

       Galswintha

They burned you!

Galswintha

       Galswintha

You do not know it

       but you're here right now

You didn't know it

but you're here right now

CAMBRIDGE

(I'M LEAVING A HOUSE IN THE CITY)

Warm

summer days

long winter nights

rolling over me

Not a care in the world

only good memories

(And some bad)

I'm leaving a house in the city

Oh bitter sweet rhymes

memories are a gift

from time

And this has been my home

Eleven years ago today

there was a

young man

in my

place

AMERICA

Our children

will be born

with blood on their hands

Hungry, not part of

and not wanting to be part of

an America

that no longer belongs to them

Have you been to the new west?

The lines were drawn more than a

decade ago

Only to redefine themselves

in "us and them"

In America

each of us

has one foot

in the Jungle

HARMONY

Cacophonous polyphony

perpetrated dissonance

Discord

A system of chaos

(random chaos as a system imposed

onto chaos)

And the systems collapse...

A

Tyranny

of blissful sound/noise

The music of sound

versus

The sound of music

The

sound of industrial civilization

grinding

to an undramatic halt

("To understand harmony one must first

investigate discord"   -Plato)

MELANCHOLY

Melancholy is a Lady

Nine sisters

awaiting

in a row

Oh Mother Mary tell me

What does a Virgin know?

Lady of the fountain

Is the Great North Sea

yet salt?

Bells upon

the mountain

Pity wind

who bears the guilt

Carry a lantern

into darkness

And to your temple of the Sun

Follow Orion

to the water

Angels from on high despair!

Look down in graceless awe

Vanity and Envy named

Dare tell me the law?

Honor to our Lady

or she may forsake us all

Speak your love

in silence

Or the magic will be gone

BLACK RAIN

The clock strikes twelve

And it's magic

Dancing two-by-two

Into never-neverland

It's only

you and me

On a darkened sea

Black rain falling down

Send a call

    to the stranded

To the ones

    who's ship

        will not set sail

It's only you and me

    on a darkened sea

        Black rain

            falling down

SNOWDONIA

I gave her

    Amber

        from Cambria

To etch in light

    And Wales is grey slate

VORTIGERN

Golden witch

    In a crimson gown

To wed the fox

    In the lair of hounds

Unleash the hordes

    Up and down

        the shore

The wolves

Have crossed

the threshold door

In Lyonesse

A song

is sung

Of wasted youth

And wicked love

A chalice of wine

For the beggar host

The Dragon fades

To become a ghost

NIGHT WIND

Lord

    of Darkness

Prince of Night

    Scatter my soul

        On the wind tonight

Let me leave

    from

        where

I am

And on dawn's mist

return again...

SANCTUARY

To seek sanctuary

and find

only isolation

To have existed

in the bowels of hell

And to ascend

to a loftier place

This I claim

Wind blown isolation

Sanctuary moves

    and the dancers promenade

I do not pity myself

but there can be no satisfaction

In the wasting of youth

    I mourn

        the passing

The going

    from this

        into that

I do not think

    that I am afraid

        of death

But I curse

    my own

        human frailty

To seek sanctuary

    and find

        only isolation

And the dancers promenade

    I am afraid of life

        or at least what

the future

may hold

If we

can not sleep

The madness

or

Shake ourselves

from this stupor

We are finished

We will have

Made our own

end

To write

To paint

To make of wood

or stone

Poetry

Music

Dance

Theater

The sciences

These are

our achievements

We need not be

the architects

of our own doom

Sanctuary

Isolation

and the dancers promenade

I mourn the passing

of this world

RIDERS

I remember

the day

the riders

came to town

On a cloud of dust

to inform us

that Richmond

had fallen

to the Yankees

I remember

    sitting on

        my grandfather's knee

And him

    telling me

        it was

            a holy war

I guess all wars are holy

    When Lee

        surrendered

    At Appomattox Courthouse

        They let them

        keep their horses

ANARCHY

And then

    night

        descended

    upon the world

Winter everywhere

    the crops

        failed in the fields

    of the country

and the live stock

Died in the throes of agony

Anarchy and brutality

in all

the cities

Hungry mobs

roamed

the streets

THE TRAIN

Go

    to warn

        the world

of a hell-bound train

    with the voice

        of children

THE WISH

I made a wish

    upon a

        falling star

Under the arbor

    of my mother's garden

    Your

        Vows

Assure

a loyal friend

The memory

of your face

And how easy

laughter came

Your strength

FIRE CHAMPION

Fire Champion

She whispers to me

in the morning

Sister of

the echo

and the mirage

She is fair

and will

embrace the winner

Fall down on your knees

Fire Champion

Seek her at

the highest level

of mountains

Take her hand

and walk

the floor

of oceans

Sire her

a son

Oh Fire Champion

GOTHIC MANIFESTO

From the abyss of centuries

Prostrate on the edge of Doomed Rebellion

We declare Mutiny!

Above the tempests of cacophony

And the tasteless vulgarity

We announce Androgyny!

Today to you Vagabonds, Whores,

Gamblers, and Thieves

To you Insurgents to whom Art is Mystery

Join us in proclaiming our Revulsion!

Enveloped in the folds of

Intoxicating Melancholy

Tethered before the Gates of the

Unknown future

We will celebrate the Classical

And seek sanctuary in the Archaic

Let us revel in our Pagan Past

Cloak ourselves in Darkness

And wear as a Badge of Honor

The title Gothic

EPITAPH

EN MA FIN EST MON COMMENCEMENT

Marco Undersong is a singer-songwriter and musician from Seattle.

He has been a member of the Pacific Northwest's Goth music scene for nearly 30 years: from his involvement with Black Atmosphere in the '90s, to his many solo enterprises, and now with the band Way Out West.

Prior to Seattle, UnderSong was on the pulse of Goth and romanticism in rock music across the US, beginning with his band The UnderSongs in San Francisco in the '70s.

Poetry has always been an integral part to UnderSong's composition, which he adopts as lyrics. Over time, however, he has written a number of poems that are best experienced in a literary context. Now, for the first time, UnderSong is sharing this work.

For a sample of how lyric poetry has influenced his musical career, visit https://marcoundersong.bandcamp.com/music or click the QR code below: